THE GATE CALLED BE

Beautiful
Is what they call the gate
My friends carry me there
And there I wait
For passersby to give alms
They better not be late
They drop silver and gold
Into my plate
Until two men came up
And changed my fate
One took my hand
And my lameness abate
I danced and I leapt
I walked real straight
Now, my life is beautiful
I feel love, not hate
As I serve a God
A God who is great

2/19/2021

HE IS

He is omnipresent
He's everywhere
He loves the world
He's always there

He is omnificent
He creates all things
He speaks His word
And new life He brings

He is Omniscient
He knows all things
He already knows
What tomorrow brings

He is Omnipotent
All powerful
He is the Creator
So wonderful

He is the beginning
He is the end
He is my counselor
He is my friend

Alpha and Omega
Knows the end from the start
He lives in our spirit
He lives in our heart

He is the lily of the valley
Rose of Sharon too
He came to save me
He came to save you

He keeps His eye on the sparrow
Dresses the lilies of the field
He makes the windstorms stop
Says peace be still

He loves me so
He died for me
He healed my body
He set me free

Continued

One day I'm going to
See Him again
Be united with
My best friend

Until that day
I will praise His name
His name is Jesus
I'll never be the same

He walks with me
And He talks with me
I'll sing to Him
Sweet melodies

I clap my hands
And I stomp my feet
Sometimes I may fast
And do not eat

I do this all
To worship Him
Without Him life
Would be so grim

But with Him
The light shines so bright
He is the Way
The Truth and the Life

1/31/2021

TWO THOUSAND YEARS AGO

2000 years ago
You gave us your Son
2000 years ago
You said He was the one

2000 years ago
You came to the Earth
2000 years ago
When Mary gave birth

2000 years ago
You saved us from sin
2000 years ago
You made us your kin

2000 years ago
You came into this world
2000 years ago
For every boy and girl

2000 years ago
You died on a cross
2000 years ago
To find those who were lost

2000 years ago
You rose from the grave
2000 years ago
To give us a chance to be saved

2000 years ago
You came from above
2000 years ago
To show us true love

2000 years later
We study and we learn
2000 years later
We await your return

4/28/2022

HE IS THE WAY, THE TRUTH, AND THE LIFE

We as human beings
Go through some trying things
But nothing compares to the joy
That the Savior brings

We as boys and girls
Face trials and turmoil
But nothing's too much
For the Lord of the world

We as man and wife
May face struggle and strife
But through the birth of a child
He gives us new life

We as young and old
Chase silver and gold
But no riches compare
To the love that He holds

We as black and white
May fuss and fight
But just as long as we remember
That He is the Way, the Truth, and the Life

He is the Way
He is the Truth
He is the Life
He is perfect in my sight

He is the Way
He is the Truth
He is the Life
He is everything that's right

These are the end times
I'm ready to fight
He is the Way and the Truth
He is the Life

7/20/2001

THE GREAT PHYSCIAN

God is the Great Physician
He'll heal your affliction
Improve your condition
Write your prescription

He is the Great I Am
The world is in His hand
He'll heal the weary land
Make the world understand

God will provide
He'll keep you alive
He'll help you survive
He'll make you to thrive

God will sustain
He'll help you maintain
And long as faith, you retain
And from sin, you refrain

God will nourish
He'll help you to flourish
Foolishness, ignore it
Wickedness, abhor it

God supports you
And courts you
Always enhances
And never thwarts you

God is love
Sent from above
Woos like a suitor
Coos like a dove

12/24/2019

LET GO. LET GOD.

When life gets hard
Let go and let God
Let down your guard
Let go and let God

Let go of control
Let God console
Let God play His role
Captain of your soul

When life is cold
Let God be bold
When life takes its toll
Let God make you whole

Let life unfold
His hand, you'll hold
He'll make you and mold
Turn you to pure gold

When life gets rough
You've had enough
With all life's stuff
When life gets tough

When you get low
It's time to let go
When life gets hard
Let go and let God

1/21/2025

THE SHOW

I am a character
In God's play
I have free will
But He has the last say

Life is His book
The world is His stage
To see what comes next
Just turn the page

He has written the story
He knows how it begins
He was there when it started
He'll be there when it ends

He has set the scene
He watches from afar
He has cast the movie
And we are the stars

He knows the plot
He has finished the script
He has chosen the actors
And we are it

He is the author of our lives
We shine like the sun
The cameras are rolling
The show must go on

10/24/2019

SCRIPTURE

The script that is Scripture
Give you your lines to say
It orders your steps
It shows you the way
It shows you how to act
In God's divine play

The script that is Scripture
It a prescription written for you
It shows you how to heal
It tells you what to do
The Master Physician gives fresh mercies
Each morning anew

His mercies are refreshing
Like morning dew
He wrote the Scriptures
For me and for you
For us to have His Word
And to know what is true

1/28/2021

HAVE YOU EVER

Have you ever had
A problem or two
And you did not know
What to say or to do

Have you ever had
A decision to make
And you did not know
Which road to take

Have you ever had
A problem to solve
And you did not know
How it would be resolved

Well let me tell you about a God
You can tell all your problems to
He'll help you find your way
So you'll know the right thing to do

Let me tell you about a God
Who knows the beginning and the end
He'll help you stay on the right path
He'll walk with you as a friend

His name is Jesus
He is the solution to every problem
No matter the challenge you face
Jesus can help you solve it

09/12/2020

GOD IS

God is the creator
He'll give you eternal life

God is the incubator
Protecting you from all strife

God is the heart regulator
Teaching you wrong from right

God is the corrector
His Word can cut you like a knife

God is the protector
He'll love you like a wife

10/24/2019

THE LORD'S LOVE

The Lord's love is iron clad
He won't forsake me, not a tad

He won't abandon me when I am bad
He will encourage me when I am sad

His love is eternal. It is not a fad
He is slow to anger or to get mad

Unto me riches, He will add
He brings me joy. He makes me glad

He is my mother. He is my dad
He is the best friend I have ever had.

3/24/2020

TOO OLD TO TRUST

I'm too old to trust
I've already done the math
I'm too old to trust
God, please don't make me laugh

I'm too old to trust
I've already walked my path
I'm too old to trust
I've thrown the baby out with the bath

I don't mean to fuss
I've given all I have
Sometimes I want to cuss
God knows I get mad

I'm too old to trust
But God has a promise to keep
I'm old, but I must
Believe Him when He speaks

2/17/2024

THE REHAB OF RAHAB

To the house of Rahab
Is where Joshua sent the spies
To scout out the land of Canaan
Where the Children of Israel were despised

They went onto the rooftop
Where under flax leaves they did hide
When they asked her where they were hidden
Rahab did not tell them, but she lied

That may seem like it was wrong
But the God of Israel was her guide
For if she would have told them
Then her family would have died

She'd go on to give birth to Boaz
Who would be her joy and pride
Which generations later would come the Christ
And the church would be His bride

Rahab was a harlot
But one day she did decide
To serve the God of Israel
And with Him, she would abide

If God can take a harlot
And love her with arms open wide
He'll do the same for you
And He'll always be by your side

2/22/2023

ON BEHALF OF NAOMI

My name was Naomi
Until grief found me
Then I became Mara
Don't know if I'll see tomorrow

I renamed myself Mara
Which means sorrow
Don't know how I'll make it
May have to beg and borrow

Until my daughter-in-law
By the name of Ruth
Said, 'your people are my people'
And showed me the truth

Of how true friendship
Can really be
And how true love
Can set you free

Then one day, we met my kinsmen
Boaz was his name
For Ruth he carried a flame
Her life would never be the same

Boaz, the redeemer
Took Ruth to be his wife
She went from being in strife
To being with the love of her life

Mother. Daughter
Sister. Friend
Hold on 'til you meet
Your redeemer kinsmen

5/11/2024

BATHSHEBA'S BATH

She bathed on the rooftop
She thought she was alone
She did not know the king was watching
All the men were supposed to be gone

He gazed at her from the rooftop
He was not supposed to be at home
He was supposed to be on the battlefield
But on the rooftop, he did not belong

He sent for her husband Uriah
And sent him to the front of the war zone
King David wanted him killed
He sent out the order from his throne

Uriah was killed on the battlefield
And King David knew he was wrong
But he wanted Bathsheba so bad
And he continued to carry on

Bathsheba had his baby
But the baby did not live long
And now the mighty king was weakened
Where he used to be so strong

Yet David loved the Lord
He wrote psalms and sang a song
He was a man after God's own heart
It was God's plan all along

2/18/2024

FOUNDATIONAL LOVE

Love is the Foundation
Upon which to build
A united state
A nation

Love is the Foundation
Upon which to build
Husband, wife
A relation

Love is the Foundation
Upon which to build
Parishioner, pastor
A congregation

Love is the Foundation
Upon which to build
You, me
Creation

Christ is the Foundation
Upon which to build
Love, hope
Salvation

12/27/2019

CONSCIOUSLY AWARE

How do I know that God is there?

How do I know that He does care?

How do I know that God is fair?

How do I know that my burdens He will bear?

How do I know that He hears my every prayer?

How do I know that He is everywhere?

All of this I know, for I am consciously aware.

8/18/2018

THE VISION

God has given me the vision
He has given me the dream
I see it like a movie
Up on the picture screen

I am on the road to success
I am on a certain path
I am guaranteed to win
God has already done the math

He has sent me on a task
He has sent me on a mission
To know the next step to take
He gives me a premonition

To live in my purpose
That is the goal
To fulfill my destiny
Is to satisfy my soul

6/5/2021

MY PURPOSE

Why did God create me?
Who am I meant to be?
What purpose did He have in mind?
When He created me to be?
Why did God create me?
What vision did He see?
What did He speak into the universe?
When He created me to be?
Why did God create me?
What beauty did He seek?
What treasure did He wish to find
When He created me to be?
Why did God create me?
What future did He foresee?
And what do I have to do in kind
To reach my destiny?
Why did God create me?
I think the answers clear
To love, be loved, and be a blessing to all
Is the reason I am here
5/18/2018

MY CREATOR

Why was I created
I'll ask my creator
Why was I made
I'll ask my maker
On what canvas was I painted
I'll ask the painter
In which gallery am I displayed
I'll ask the curator
How will I grow
I'll ask the incubator
How will my story go
I'll ask the narrator
How will I be made free
I'll ask the liberator
How will my thoughts be managed
I'll ask the mind regulator
Who will speak to my heart
I'll ask the master communicator
Who will inspire me
I'll ask my motivator
How high will I go
I'll ask my elevator
Where will I travel
I'll ask my navigator
How high will I fly
I'll ask my aviator
Who will save me, I asked
He answered, "Jesus, the Savior"

11/26/2018

GIFTS

Unwrap your gifts
Do not keep them under wraps
God gave you gifts to share with others
To improve their lives perhaps

Unwrap your gifts
Do not keep them under wraps
God gave you gifts to guide other people
Who can use them as a map

Unwrap your gifts
Do not keep them under wraps
God gave you gifts to fulfill the needs of others
To fill in some of their gaps

Unwrap your gifts
Do not keep them under wraps
God gave you the gifts to give to others
Until you have nothing left

5/18/2018

WHAT ARE YOUR GIFTS?

What are your gifts?
Let's take inventory

What are your gifts?
What is in your repository?

What are your gifts?
Do they tell your story?

What are your gifts?
Do they increase your territory?

To find your gifts
You should be exploratory

Then, share your gifts
And to God be the glory

2/23/2019

YOUR GIFT

Your gift is free
Free from the Lord
So don't worry about money
And your gift, do not hoard

Be a good steward of your talent
Do not let it come back void
Cultivate your strengths
Or they shall be destroyed

So share your gift with others
Before you return to the sky
And make the Lord happy
That He gave you his supply

2/22/2019

LIVING OUT LOUD

I may be bruised
Living under a cloud
But I'm not stopping
I am living out loud

I may be broken
Not standing out in a crowd
But I'm still here
Living out loud

And I am better, not bitter
And for that I am proud
I keep pressing forward
I am living out loud

And to God be the glory
I keep my head bowed
For I am eternally grateful
I am living out loud

4/21/2018

Made in the USA
Columbia, SC
13 March 2025